TRUSTING
GOD WHEN IT
HURTS

Hope When Your Life Falls Apart

TRUSTING
GOD WHEN IT
HURTS

Hope When Your Life Falls Apart

PRESENTED BY

JILL BRISCOE

COMPILED BY
SHELLY ESSER

Just Between Us magazine, Brookfield, Wisconsin 53045

TRUSTING GOD WHEN IT HURTS

Printed in the United States of America

This book is part of a series on relevant topics for *Just Between Us*. For more information about *Just Between Us* magazine, please turn to the back of this book.

Unless otherwise noted, Scripture quotations are taken from the Holy Bible: New International Version®. Copyright © 1973, 1978, 1984 by International Bible Society.

The Team: Suzan Braun, Kate Habrel, Jeanette Kay, Nancy Krull, Debbie Leech, Mary Perso

Cover & Layout Design: Sophie Beck

just between us

TRUSTING
GOD WHEN IT HURTS

The pain brought on by trials is often paralyzing. Fear, bitterness, anger, and doubt can cause us to forget that within our places of struggle and suffering–GOD is there, providing hope and grace. Asking us to trust in Him, He is there to remind us that we are not alone. In these ten inspiring chapters, women share their journeys of pain and faith, sharing God's provision and care during times of darkness–revealing the treasures that God can bring into our lives during these difficult seasons.

1

Bringing Faith Home

How one woman broke through her unbelief and doubt in the face of tragedy.

by Tammy Kill

May 22, 2011–the day our lives would change forever and our faith would be tested in the valley of pain and despair. Even with all the tragedies, deaths, and trials I have experienced in the past, this test would prove too much for my faith to bear. This day would be the starting point in a journey from that point of despair to bringing *Faith* home again.

Sundays are supposed to be the day of rest, right? For the Kill family of 10, it is usually met with a battle of wills, getting dressed, hairdos, and rushing to get to church. There we attempt to enjoy the message as we make countless trips to the nursery and bathroom with our twins (four-year-old Faith and Joy), and our youngest, rambunctious two-year-old Gary. For us, Sundays are not the day of rest, but more like the "day of test," one we usually fail at miserably in the area of patience and longsuffering.

On this particular Sunday it was just the kids and me, as my husband of 18 years was at work. Gary has been a funeral director in our town of Lima, Ohio, for 17 years. His job often requires that he work on Sundays. I had the weekend off from my job as a hospice nurse (yes, I know...funeral director, hospice nurse, last name Kill...crazy!).

After returning home that day, I found myself able to take a nap while little Gary took his. It seemed that God was giving me a chance to catch up on some much needed sleep.

When Gary arrived home around five, I already had that dreaded honey-do list waiting for him, which included mowing the lawn. I then headed to church to prepare for the upcoming Vacation Bible school. I was excited over what God was doing and the vision He had poured into my heart.

As I pulled out of the driveway, my sweet little Faith came running out of the house, "Mommy, please don't go!" I looked over to see Gary in the garage filling up a tire on that old green lawnmower with that same disappointed look as I left. Once again I was torn between ministry and family. It's hard to always know what is right.

As I headed to church, my heart ached. Arriving at church, I prepared for the arrival of the youth group. Within minutes I got a call. It is the call that stopped everything. Suddenly, nothing else mattered as I picked up the phone and heard my older daughter Hope scream, "Mom, Faith was run over by the lawnmower!" Devastated and shocked at such horrifying words, I felt unable to fully comprehend what I was hearing.

I cannot express what the rest of that day was like. A mad dash home produced absolute terror, as I took in the sight of my husband in the yard kneeling over the mangled body of our little girl. "Faith!...Gary!" Both her feet were cut, as was a very large portion of her left leg and groin area. Blood everywhere. To use the word my husband said over and over that day, "carnage."

The next few hours were a fight not only to save our little girl's leg, but also her life. We almost lost her. To add to the severity and the impossible devastation my husband had to bear, Faith never passed out...she knew and felt everything.

Faith went by life-flight to Nationwide Children's Hospital in Columbus, spending that night in surgery, stabilizing her and saving her leg. We had no assurance she would ever walk again. We just tried to keep our minds focused enough to function for her. How could we ever process this? Gary was in shock. I later learned that Faith had walked up behind her father as he was backing up the mower. Gary had seen her playing safely on the other side of the yard moments earlier. Then the engine stalled, and there she was. It was a horrible accident, no one to blame, but unbearable all the same.

Faith underwent 12 surgeries to graft her leg and feet. I watched as this frail little body was wracked with pain and depression. I've never seen a four year old depressed. She would ask me, "Mommy, when will I walk again?" All I could say was, "soon."

The real truth was I did not have an answer. I want to say that I held on during this time, that I was able to see the miracles we witnessed over and over again, even from the beginning with God choosing to spare her life. The truth is I didn't know if I believed Him anymore, or if I even wanted to. I was trying my best to put on a good face; but as Faith slowly started to recover, I got sicker and sicker in my heart.

Faith suffered many setbacks on her road to recovery. At week six I started to notice blisters forming around the wound on her leg. I feared the worst; and of course that fear was realized–a staph infection!

The day of Faith's twelfth surgery, I was sitting alone at her bedside. I was agonizing over a surgeon's decision to put the graft over her leg with the staph infection still present. I found myself, for the first time since those first few emergent days of the accident, pleading with God. It was then I realized…"God, I'm mad!" I hadn't been able to pray, read, or have much time to even think about my feelings toward God. In fact, I found every time I was having a thought of wanting to pray, I would keep myself busy.

In that moment, I finally turned to God. "Lord, only You and I know how I'm feeling. Here is my battered, depressed, and beaten-down child. She's in a constant state of physical and emotional pain, and there's nothing I can do for her. Please, please do not let them do this surgery today!"

I realized then why I couldn't pray. The Wednesday before the accident, I had a dream. I saw one of my children, with life-threatening wounds over much of her body…then the accident happened. Was that God somehow warning me? Was that the enemy? I couldn't figure it out. What I did know was that if God, my Friend, my Father, the God of miracles, the One I lean on and go to in that private place of intercession was the same God that knew this before it happened and had let it happen anyway, how could I ever trust and love Him again?

So there I was, full of doubt and no possible way of showing Faith *any* kind of faith. Yet there, in the stillness of that room, God knew I was angry…and He was okay with that. A song flooded into my heart…

Holding onto Faith

Holding onto Hope

Holding onto promises I've trusted were enough

But what do you do when you don't feel it

What do you do when you don't see it

You hold onto Faith.

Miraculously, the grafting didn't take place that day. The nurse said the surgeon was running late, so he would clean the wound again and wait for the following week!

As the weeks turned into months of therapy, Faith came home once again in a wheelchair, and then a walker, and by Christmas only a slight limp was visible. The scars are still very evident, but so are the miracles!

Hebrews 11:1 says, "Now faith is the substance of things hoped for, the evidence of things not seen" (KJV). Faith IS the substance, the reason we can hope. Hope not for a way out of our troubles, but a way by His grace to get through them. There is light at the end of a very dark tunnel that I must walk through with no way to escape. There the joy, peace, victory, and yes, *faith* are all waiting on the other side. Now I'm seeing there may be no way to truly experience those supernatural things in this life, those things we can't see, until we have gone through those times of soul-wrenching pain.

God knows all-too-well the grief of seeing a child in pain. He was there then and He is here now, waiting patiently on you and me. Through this tragedy, I learned that God was not only bringing our daughter back home to us, but even more than that, He was bringing faith home again into our hearts.

2

How to Comfort Job

Having a ministry of presence.

by Jill Briscoe

Have you ever lost someone close to you? Perhaps they lived far away, yet you found yourself saying, "I have to go." So you packed a bag and traveled, maybe a considerable distance, just to be there with family and friends. And what happened when you arrived? You were greeted at the door, and you simply said, "I had to come." And somehow that was enough.

I was privileged to serve on the board of World Relief, a Christian agency. Their aim is to relieve suffering worldwide in the name of Christ. One summer they invited me to go to Croatia, just after the conflict with Serbia. This was during a period of uneasy peace. I joined a dozen other Christian women, and off we went. "What will we do when we get there?" we asked each other. We didn't know, but we met together at a specified place and traveled to Croatia to sympathize and comfort. The experience turned out to be life–changing.

That summer on the border of Serbia, we women met refugees–Croats, Serbs, and Muslims who, fresh from the horrors of war, told us their stories. We listened, took part in meetings, visited the camps, and did various practical things. But mostly we kept saying, "We just had to come!" Over and over again they thanked us for "just being there." We learned that you have to get close enough to comfort and that it will cost you. It will cost you time, possibly money, and it will most certainly involve some creative enterprise.

LET YOUR TEARS TALK

Once Job's friends had come close enough to comfort, they expressed their deep concern in the custom of their culture: "When they saw him from a distance... they began to weep aloud" (Job 2:12). They let their tears talk. No one said a word to him because they saw how great his suffering was.

Can you cry? Sometimes I can and sometimes I can't. I have discovered, as I have traveled "my Father's world that broke my Father's heart," that my Father's heart lives within me in the person of the Holy Spirit. I have learned to ask Him to pray for the hurting who need help with "such feeling that it cannot be expressed in words" (Rom. 8:26, TLB). There is a groaning and a grieving that expresses itself in tears that only the Holy Spirit can produce in us. These are not crocodile tears but Christ's tears.

I have been on the receiving end of such empathy too. I remember becoming hard and embittered because I was lonely. My husband's work took him away from the family for months on end. I knew I needed to talk to someone, but to whom? My senior missionary's husband traveled too, even more than mine. She seemed to be doing just fine! How could I possibly share my pain with her? She was sure to open her Bible and point me to some sacrificial text of Scripture that would emphasize my lack of spirituality. This situation was not what I expected when we left the business world to join a mission. After a miserable few weeks on that particular ash heap of my dreams, I summoned up my courage and went to talk to my "model" of sufficiency.

I remember entering her office and seeing her toiling over mounds of paperwork. She was stretched to the limit with the responsibilities she carried and was busy like nobody else I knew. I felt guilty bothering her. She glanced up and saw, in the words of Job, "how great my suffering was." Immediately she put her pen down, turned her chair around, and gave me her full attention. She knew from years of experience that listening is akin to loving. Her body language said to me, "You are center stage in my thinking–talk to me!"

I burst out then with my complaint. I told her I was fed up with the "Daddy space" in my children's lives. That I had tried to follow her example and be the perfect little missionary wife, but it hadn't worked. "I know you'll find this difficult to understand," I blurted out, "because you've been able to be all the things you should be and find joy in it, but I only find pain." I stopped then and looked at her. I couldn't believe my eyes. She was crying, really crying. "It's hard, isn't it," she said simply, reaching for the tissues.

But it wasn't those words that shouted out to me; it was her tears. The sound of tears talking cannot be escaped. "I can't believe I'm seeing what I'm seeing," I muttered. "You mean it's been hard for you too?" She laughed then, inviting me to sit down. Her sympathetic silence had encouraged me to tell her what was troubling me, but her tears told me it was all right to feel as I did. More than that, her tears told me that she felt the pain too. Her genuine concern assured me there was someone who had been there and survived, and that there could be victory and joy in the lonely times for me as well. It strikes me that all of us can probably do these two simple things for our friends. We can have a ministry of presence, and we can let our tears talk.

We are often so overwhelmed by the idea of seeing someone we love who is very ill–perhaps undergoing cancer treatment–or one who has been recently bereaved, that we tend to keep our distance. It's easier that way. Maybe we are willing to go but are intimidated by the thought of having to say something once we get there. *I'm not qualified enough, spiritual enough, experienced enough,* we tell ourselves. *Perhaps I'll say the wrong thing and make matters worse.* Yet Job's friends went and expressed their concern their way. We can at least attempt to do the same. Perhaps it would not be appropriate for us to tear our robes, cry aloud, and sprinkle dust on our heads as they did, but we can put our arms around Job, his wife, or his children and do it in the way most suited to our personalities and situations. We can find ways to "weep with those that weep."

SIGNIFICANT SILENCE

The friends, at least, took the trouble to visit Job's ash heap and sit on it with him; that was not a comfortable thing to do for seven days. Remember, seven days was the period of mourning for the dead! They felt they were coming to his funeral before it happened. Once they had a good look at him, they had very little doubt that Job was not long for this world. So, "No one said a word to him, because they saw how great his suffering was" (Job 2:13). These friends were not afraid of silence.

We are so afraid of silence in our noisy culture. We believe we must fill silence with words, whether we have anything significant to say or not. And yet sometimes someone else's suffering is so intense that silence is the only appropriate response. Don't feel you have to say something. There is something all of us–young or old, clever or timid, spiritually deep or not so deep–can do. At the very least, we can go, we can cry, and we can listen lovingly. There's nothing too difficult about that, and the amazing thing is that that's exactly where the ministry of encouragement begins!

IN FOR THE LONG HAUL

Another impressive thing about Job's comforters was the fact that they were in it for the long haul. Maybe Job didn't appreciate that fact as time wore on, but at least they didn't bail out at the first opportunity. If we are going to be real comforters, we are going to have to settle in to see it through. We may not be in a position to be absent from our home or business, but we can take steps to assure Job that we'll be there till the end.

A young woman in our church lost her husband to cancer. For the first year of her loss, her friends, family, and even strangers, rallied around and ministered to her. Then came the second year–the year the experts say is usually the worst. "I hope they are right," she wrote to me, "because this second year has been the pits! It was great at first, with so many wonderful people giving me their full attention, but now they are busy with their own lives, and I'm all alone."

It's obviously not possible for everyone to keep up such intensive attention, but some should. I am learning to ask God, "Do you want me to be in this for the long haul?" Sometimes He says no, and sometimes He says yes. If He replies in the affirmative, it's extremely important to be faithful. And if we are the ones who should stick around until He says it's over, we should take steps to learn what to do and what to say. You can't stay silent forever, and you have to blow your nose and dry your eyes at some point, and then it will be time to talk. When that time comes, we had better be equal to the task. Otherwise we may earn the same rebuke Job's friends heard eventually because they had not "spoken rightly."

There can be great comfort in words. But that all depends on what the words are and when we use them. Our words should always have their base in Scripture. These are the words that can be used by the Holy Spirit to comfort and heal. They certainly should not be words of rebuke or criticism. When Job's comforters later break their silence and become his critic, we see Job's suffering intensify. After all, relational pain can be the deepest and most intense pain of all. "Sticks and stones may break my bones but words will never hurt me," the saying goes. I don't believe that, do you? Words can cut far deeper than a stone and beat one's feelings red raw. Our words need to be carefully chosen and applied to heal and help, not to hurt, even if the suffering is a result of the person's foolishness or bad choices.

Then the words need to be applied at the right time. I'm sure you have been the victim of "right" words spoken at the wrong time! Timing is vitally important when we are trying to encourage someone. Ecclesiastes 3:7 tells us that there is "a time to be silent and a time to speak."

I remember working with a young teenager. She had been promiscuous before she found the Lord and had very little home support once she became a believer. She struggled on but fell into her old ways again. One day she came to tell us she was pregnant and her parents wouldn't let her come home. I remember feeling pretty exasperated, looking at her standing on our doorstep. She knew better. She had seemed to really put things together, had gotten a job, and had begun to turn her life around. How could she have been so foolish? And if she was going to have sex, why didn't she take precautions? Things needed saying, but not then. Now, in her extremity, she needed a bath, a meal, a hug, and a bed! So I tried only to use wise words of welcome and told her I was so glad she had felt able to come to us in her trouble. That night, that was enough. There would be a time in the future when she would be ready to receive my words, but it wasn't now.

There is a difference between constructive and destructive criticism. Real love always looks for a way of being constructive. When Job's friends began to talk, they undid much of the good they had done. They began to accuse him and thereby did the devil's work for him.

Next time you come alongside a friend or family member in pain, remember the ministry of presence—let your tears do the talking!

3

Sustaining Grace

Trusting God to give you strength for each day.

by Shelly Esser

One of my favorite books is *The Hiding Place* by Corrie ten Boom. I'll never forget the thrill as a young teenager of actually getting to see her in person. It was one of the highlights of my life. God recently brought to mind a heartfelt exchange in the book between Corrie and her father, when she was a young girl. Corrie was upset thinking about her father dying someday. As was his habit, he sat down at the edge of her bed to tuck her in.

"Corrie," he began gently, "when you and I go to Amsterdam—when do I give you your ticket?"

Corrie sniffed a few times, "Why, just before we get on the train."

"Exactly. And our wise Father in heaven knows when we're going to need things, too. Don't rush ahead of Him. When the time comes... you will look into your heart and find the strength you need—just in time."

That moment in the book came flooding back to my memory while we were about to get on a train that was completely unfamiliar to us and that we were unprepared for. Our lively 13-year-old daughter was facing serious surgery. I heard my Heavenly Father's whisper amidst my fears, "When will I give you the ticket?"

"When I get on the train." And as we were just about to board the train, watching the daughter we loved being wheeled into surgery, God gave us the ticket we needed—a ticket overflowing with grace, a supernatural strength enabling us to deal with the moment at hand, passengers He provided to come along with support for the journey, and a grace that enabled us to know that it can be well with our souls even when it's not well with our circumstances. Your loving Father knows all about your present circumstances and need and is waiting to hand you the ticket. His supply never runs dry; it is never overburdened. He is never surprised. Interestingly, He doesn't promise help before help is needed. No—when we are on the edge of our need—His hand is stretched out.

Now almost five months after our daughter's surgery, she has still not fully recovered. Emotionally draining long days are filled with chronic pain, confusion, a lack of acceptable answers, more medical tests, and endless doctor's appointments, but God continues to remind me of the ticket. As the Conductor of our lives, He knows the way of the journey we take. He sees the bends in the track and the dark tunnels ahead. Daily, I hold on to the knowledge that God is ever present, and that especially as a mom of a suffering child, He has given me what author and speaker Jennifer Rothschild calls "spectator grace." A special grace for those of us who have to watch the ones we love walk with pain and difficulty.

My mind has raced back through the years of difficult trains we have boarded before. Without exception, God provided the ticket. He has seen us *through*. I know this time will be no different. That reality keeps me going. "I have summoned you by name; you are mine. *When* you pass through the waters, I will be with you; and *when* you pass through the rivers, they will not sweep over you. *When* you walk through the fire, you will not be burned; the flames will not set you ablaze. For I am the LORD, your God..." (Isa. 43:1-3, italics mine). We must get on the train and into the journey before we can claim the promise. *When* we get on the train His presence is there; He walks with us. God also continued to give us "crisis grace" as we walked through our daughter's illness. In the trials is where His power and work are displayed best–in the tough spot that tries our faith, because true faith counts on God and believes before it sees. This faith sustains us in the most trying places, when everything around us seems to contradict God's Word. "I am still confident of this: I will see the goodness of the Lord in the land of the living. Wait for the LORD; be strong and take heart and wait for the Lord" (Psa. 27:13-14).

We are waiting. We have not yet reached our destination–for whatever reason it's not time for us to get off the train. I don't know what's around the bend, where this journey intends to take us. I do know that God's ticket of grace continues to be sufficient in this place. And in the words of Father ten Boom, "our wise Father in heaven knows when we're going to need things. When the time comes, you will look into your heart and find the strength you need–just in time."

4

Praying When Life Gets Hard

How to pray when your life is overwhelming.

by Nancy Nordenson

In a dimly lit hospital room, I stared out the window into the early morning darkness and waited for the drips of IV fluid to begin the contractions that would birth my lifeless midterm baby. My sorrow was lonely and deep. I wanted to pray, but there were no words to voice the thoughts that swirled in my mind.

When life is hard, prayer is hard. Grief, illness, depression, and anger invade our lives and hang on with tenacity, stealing our desire to pray and our belief in prayer just when we need them most. Physically and emotionally weary, we struggle to move from "Dear God" to "Amen." Simply getting through the day becomes our goal, leaving the luxury of connecting with God for better times.

I find it difficult to meet the expectations of Scripture regarding prayer. I fail to pray "with thanksgiving" (Phil. 4:6) when the situation I've prayed about for so long is only getting worse. How many of us pray "without ceasing" (1 Thess. 5:17, KJV) when waves of grief knock us over, pull us down, and hold us under? When disappointment and anger over dashed plans and failed relationships consume our thoughts and our unquiet hearts, where do we find the emotional energy to pray?

But God commands that we pray. He didn't make prayer optional; He doesn't hand us a signed excuse, releasing us from prayer, when life becomes difficult. God must have known that the process of thinking thoughts to an unseen "Something" might seem inadequate in the face of our own suffering, that spending time alone in our room, praying the same thing yet again, might seem better spent pacing. He must have known each of us would come to the difficult day when, faced with the urge or challenge to pray, we would instead say, "I just can't," and go no further.

In obedience to God's command, prayer must become what Oswald Chambers called "an effort of the will." When life is difficult, any effort can seem like too much. But if we explore ways of praying that may be easier with limited physical and emotional strength, we more readily may set our wills in the direction of prayer.

FIND A PRAYERFUL PLACE.

Jesus often went to solitary places to pray, such as the mountaintop, the lake, and the garden (see Matt.14:23, 26:36-46, Mark1:35; and John 6:22-24). We can't always arrange a trip to a mountaintop, but we can find somewhere appealing to pray. Slip into a church sanctuary, and look at the cross or stained-glass windows. Spend a quiet hour at a museum. Create a prayerful place in your home by lighting a candle or placing your chair by the window. Or simply go for a walk.

USE OTHERS' WORDS.

When our prayers need words we can't seem to find, we can use someone else's. The Bible is filled with prayers. Consider the petitions of Moses as he struggled to lead God's people. Listen to the kings of Israel as they prayed for help in battle. Borrow the words of the psalmists as they prayed for deliverance, protection, and forgiveness. In the New Testament, meditate on the words of Jesus and the apostles.

For example, consider the prayer of King Jehoshaphat. A messenger greeted him with these words: "A vast army is coming against you" (2 Chron. 20:2). The future of his kingdom was in peril; he and his people were trapped by mighty opponents. The king listened to this message and then prayed: "We have no power to face this vast army that is attacking us. We do not know what to do, but our eyes are upon you" (v.12). I've borrowed these words of the besieged king when I've felt overpowered by circumstances outside of my control. His prayer is like a flare shot up to the God who rescues.

Consider using other written prayers as well, such as the words from hymns or from a book of prayers.

MEDITATE ON JESUS' LIFE.

Jesus had a hard life. Can we find something in His life that mirrors our own difficult times? The gospels tell us about the time He prayed alone at night, so full of emotion that He sweat drops of blood. We can read about the betrayal by His friends and the religious establishment. We can wonder how He must have suffered over being misunderstood by His family.

Did He feel sorrow when He was rebuked rather than praised for performing a miracle? What was He thinking as He wept over His friend Lazarus's grave? How did He find the strength to put one foot in front of the other on the way to His own crucifixion? Can we relate to His cry on the cross, "My God, why have you forsaken me" (Matt. 27:46)?

Feeling scared and cowardly when I needed to be calm and brave, I thought about Jesus entering Jerusalem for the last time before His death. Even knowing what was ahead, Jesus walked right into His crisis. Horribly unfair things were about to happen to Him. Humiliation and death awaited. If He could walk into that, then with His strength, I could walk into the experience I was facing.

As we meditate upon Jesus' life in this way, we connect with Him and share our experience with Him. This, too, is a way of praying.

PRAY A REPEATED PHRASE.

It can also be helpful to pray often using the same few words. These words can be prayed aloud, whispered, or said inwardly while engaged in another activity.

There is no magic in the repetition of these words. Rather, what you're seeking is a continual prayer, a constant reminder of the truth to which you so desperately need to cling, a focus for unfocused thoughts. The sudden onsets of panic and grief after the loss of my baby eased when I repeated Jesus' words over and over again: "Peace I leave with you; my peace I give you" (John 14:27).

REMEMBER THE HOLY SPIRIT'S INTERCESSION.

The advocacy of the Holy Spirit on our behalf is unceasing. Paul tells us that the Holy Spirit prays for us when we are weak, when we don't even know how to pray or what to pray for (see Rom. 8:26-27).

Just as a bewildered plaintiff or defendant—without ability to plead his own case before a judge and jury—asks an attorney to speak for him, so we can entrust our cause to the Holy Spirit and remain silent for a time. This silence does not imply a lack of interest in being before God but rather a choice to be represented by the petitions of the Holy Spirit.

ASSUME A POSTURE OF PRAYER.

There is a good reason for the traditional prayer posture of closed hands and eyes: The less we see and touch, the more we focus on praying. But when our hearts and minds are racing, even this traditional prayer posture can be inadequate to help us focus. Sometimes, we may need a more intentional posture, such as kneeling or even lying prostrate on the floor. With our faces to the floor, we find ourselves in the company of others who have cried out to God from this position: Ezekiel, in despair; Ezra, ashamed and disgraced; Daniel, terrified; Jesus, sorrowful and troubled.

WRITE IT ONCE.

Simply thinking about our problems before praying may emotionally exhaust or dredge up resentment or anger. When I described to a friend my struggle to pray about a difficult situation, she advised me to write out a prayer that covered all the aspects of the problem. Then she suggested I read this prayer whenever I felt the need to pray, focusing my heart and mind on the words I'd already written. What a relief it was to have a plan for prayer, so I wouldn't need to search the pain daily, starting from scratch.

SHOW, DON'T TELL.

When Sennacherib sent a letter to King Hezekiah threatening to destroy Jerusalem, Hezekiah read it and immediately went to the temple. He spread the letter out before the Lord and began to pray (see 2 Kings 19).

Could our prayers be supported by a visual aid as well? By using images rather than words, we can bypass the energy needed to find the words. With one action we can lay our situation before the God who sees as well as hears. Spread the stack of bills, the anti-depressant prescription, or the abnormal biopsy report before Him. Tell God by showing God.

PRAY WITH YOUR TEARS.

Mary wept at Jesus' feet after the death of her brother, Lazarus (see John11:32-33). Can you recall a time when you cried with another person? Do you remember the emotional release and subsequent bonding with that person after the tears? We can open our hearts to God and deepen our relationship with Him by crying in His presence, offering our tears as prayers.

EXPRESS YOUR ANGER.

Anger blocks communication. Are you angry at God over your situation? If so, tell Him how you feel. Follow Job's example of talking to God with honesty and respect. Talk it out, write it down, and watch for His answer.

BE SILENT.

Only the best of friends can sit together silently with ease. The psalmist reminds us to "Be still, and know that I am God" (Ps. 46:10) and reassures us that "the LORD Almighty is with us" (v. 11). Allow yourself to sit silently in the presence of God.

ASK OTHERS TO PRAY.

To release God's power on the battlefield below, Moses' friends helped him hold up his staff (see Ex. 17:8-13). In the same way, the prayers of others support us and release the power of God into the battles of our lives. If you don't know of at least one person who is committed to praying for you, ask someone.

As I stared out the window in that hospital room, I had a definite sense of others praying for me. My loneliness eased and the struggle to pray relaxed. I didn't have to search for the words anymore; I knew the words of someone else would bring me before God.

DO YOU BELIEVE?

At the memorial service we held for our infant daughter, we read the words spoken by Jesus to a grieving Martha four days after the death of her brother. Jesus said to her: "'I am the resurrection and the life.... Do you believe this?' Martha replied, 'Yes, Lord'" (John 11:25-27). Jesus then proceeded to the tomb, twice overcome with emotion before arriving. Moments later Lazarus walked out of the tomb, resurrected.

Despair and belief, sorrow and joy, death and life, waiting and rescue are the threads woven together in the fabric of this story. They are also the fabric of my story and perhaps yours. As with Martha, our hope when life gets hard rests in the way we answer Jesus' question: "I am the resurrection and the life. Do you believe this?" If we can say yes, no matter how we choose to pray about the difficulties we face, we know that we leave our prayers in trustworthy hands.

5

Light in the Tunnel

God's sustaining power in the midst of a family tragedy.

by Susie O'Berski

October 28, 2010 had been a beautiful day. I was on my way home after enjoying time with friends. I decided to splurge and make my husband one of his favorite meals. We could eat and relax when he walked in the door. Then the phone rang.

His voice had a different sound to it as he calmly said we were heading to the hospital. The hospital had just called him and asked if we had a son who was a student at the university. When he answered yes, they said that Matt was in the emergency room and they couldn't wake him.

Dashing out the door, we knew the heart-wrenching impossibility of erasing the 100 miles between our house and the hospital as we responded to the call no parent ever wants. I felt sick. I took Michael's hand and we sat in silence. We prayed, lifting our youngest son up to the Lord, thankful He was with Matt when we were unable. Calling our four other sons scattered across the country, we relayed the limited information and asked them to contact everyone they knew to pray. We continued calling family and friends to cover Matt in prayer.

Amidst the panic was a quiet calm. God was reminding us that whatever happened next, Matt was okay because he was already His. An incomprehensible assurance flooded over us. Salvation had never meant so much to me before–because of Jesus and His loving grace, our 6' 3" baby boy was "okay" whether dead or alive in the eternal arms of our Heavenly Father.

When we arrived at the hospital, I felt sick again, my knees weak. We rushed in to find Matt. The hospital staff could not have been kinder to us or more caring of Matt as they tried to explain what was going on. When we entered the room, we found Matt hooked up to machines, wires everywhere, and his face badly bruised and battered–lifeless. I rushed over to him, gently took his hand and leaned in to kiss his cheek and whisper, "Mattie, Mom and Dad are here." With a gasp for air I prayed, "Oh Lord, help my baby!" Although our world had stopped, God lovingly assured us He remained on His throne, holding "our world" in His hands.

When Matt was missed at an afternoon meeting, friends and floor mates started putting the pieces together. Someone had last seen Matt at dinner 24 hours earlier. A staff member ran to check Matt's room. Unable to get inside, he called the police and together they were able to push the door open to rescue Matt, who was barely breathing. He had fallen out of his lofted bed, hit the refrigerator, and then the hard concrete floor below. From the pool of blood found there, it appeared he had crawled to the door for help where he passed out again. The worst for me was the unknown–how long had Matt lain unconscious in his room alone? Had he called out for help? Heartbroken with this thought, God's light shined brightly through my sister, Patti. She put her arms around me and reminded me Jesus had been with Matt and asked, "Who better to hold Matt, you or Jesus?"

Our family rallied and rushed to join us within the next 18 hours. Praying together ushered in His light for direction and warmth, melting the coldness of tragedy. That light continued to illuminate our way through the following days, weeks, and months.

Despite being on life support for the first couple days, Matt's prognosis seemed hopeful from the initial testing. Still in a coma, but now breathing on his own, an MRI of his brain was done on the fourth day to give a clearer picture of the damage. It was not good news. We all stood around listening in disbelief as the doctors shared their thoughts. Matt's injury had resulted in bleeding on both sides of the brain, and his diagnosis was a Severe Traumatic Brain Injury; specifically, a Diffuse Axonal Injury.

God had given us excellent, caring doctors, but as much as they wanted to tell us Matt would return to normal, they could not. They could not even assure us he would ever wake up, and if he did, what his future would look like. I was overwhelmed with this thought when Matt squeezed my hand. My heart jumped! I felt God reminding us that despite all of the dismal news, this was not too much for Him to handle–that He remained on His throne in charge of Matt and his future. God lit our lives with His hope. God handpicked our nurses and doctors, many of them Christians. God surrounded us with His family from around the world through praying, calling, emailing, and visiting. It seemed as if everyone we had ever met got the news of Matt and covered us with prayer and tremendous loving care. Indeed, every need was supplied according to His riches in Christ Jesus. Have you ever thought what God's riches in Christ Jesus means? An endless supply of God's very best, much more than we could have ever hoped or imagined! God's provision freed us to focus on Matt and energized us to lovingly care for him.

With Matt solidly connected in a wonderful church, actively involved in Young Life, and friends with everyone he ever met, our desire was to have Matt accepted into the rehab program at the University of Michigan. We saw how Matt's support group was there, not back in Kalamazoo where we had moved right after dropping him off at college as a freshman.

Indeed, God cleared the way. Still in a coma, Matt was moved to the rehab floor one week after his fall. Rehab? How? Matt was not asleep, but in a coma! I have to applaud rehab therapists. They look at someone seemingly hopeless and work tirelessly. He had to relearn how to sit, stand, walk, eat, and care for himself. God would hand me the blinders each day to help me focus and say, "Look at Me; I am your Hope." Slowly, very slowly, Matt began to respond and his favorite response by the second week was growling like a dinosaur … silly, but we were thrilled with any kind of sound! God was reminding us our hope did not lie in sounds, therapists, doctors, walking, or even health. Our hope was in God alone!

Countless times God needed to ask me, "Susan, do you trust Me? Matt is Mine." God uses His people to remind us He is the Rainbow Maker and Star Breather, encouraging us to place every moment and future moment in His hands. Matt's room was decorated with love–posters, pictures, cards, Scripture, and rainbows!

Our choosing to stay in Ann Arbor meant that Michael would have to travel back and forth to work. Thankfully, his "work" is ministry and our church family freed Michael to do whatever was needed. I quit my job on day four when we heard Matt's recovery would be measured in months. Matt would need 24/7 care for weeks with ongoing therapy, and I rejoiced that I was available!

When a crisis occurs, your world gets small and very focused–little matters except the immediate. Many days and nights I sat in Matt's room very much aware of the potentially long, dark tunnel we were going through. How did we have such peace? Perspective is determined by the source of light we choose. We chose to seek and sit in the light of Jesus!

From lifelessness to fully functioning, seven weeks later Matt walked out of the hospital! Therapy continues at home and through a cognitive therapy program with the goal of getting Matt back to school in the fall. Praising God, we walk forward, trusting His light to lead our way–a light in the tunnel!

6

A Time to Recover

Giving your mind, body, and soul time to mend.

by Shelly Esser

For some time, I had started several articles without ever finishing them. The ideas were there, but the energy was lacking. During our magazine's 20th anniversary, I was able to pull favorite articles from the last several decades. In God's goodness, He gave me a break. I was empty and tired. Having just come through a three-year health crisis with my daughter's and husband's health, I was burnt out. Until we came *through*, I didn't realize what it had taken out of me. I couldn't just go on as normal after those intense years of depletion. I had to recognize where I was at and be honest with myself and God. What was my body, spirit, and coldness of heart telling me? Unfortunately, our fast-paced culture doesn't make it okay to stop; we don't give people time or permission to *recover* from the storms of life.

Not long ago, the phone rang. It was a depleted pastor's wife who had been through breast cancer, depression, and church conflict—and she was spent. She, too, needed to *recover* from life. You can't just keep going on to the next thing. Sooner or later there will be some kind of fallout.

The realization hit me that I couldn't go on like this anymore. By opening my hands to release my exhaustion, I was also opening my hands to receive God's provision which started with an intimate knowledge of what I needed. God was whispering, "I feel your fatigue and I'm concerned about you. You need time to recover." He didn't let me escape that truth.

When people ask me now how I'm doing I say—without guilt—that I am in a time of *recovery*. For the last couple of years, I have been trying to figure out how to work through this needed phase in my life.

Scripture has many examples of recovery phases—God rested on the seventh day and Jesus after long days of draining ministry with needy people, slipped away to what? Recover! Into the hills ALONE (Matt. 14:23; Lk. 6:12). The dictionary defines *recover* as "to get back, to make up for, to regain the strength, composure or balance of, to reclaim." Recovery gives us the necessary time to regain our balance, slowly allowing God to put things back together again. Ecclesiastes 3:7 puts it another way, "There is

…a time *to mend.*"

Here are five things that have helped me as I have intentionally worked on my recovery:

1. RECOVERY IS NECESSARY.

We need to see the importance of allowing God to restore. Jesus said in Matt. 11:28, "Come to me, all you who are weary and burdened, and I will give you rest." Psalm 23:2-3, "…He leads me beside quiet waters, He restores my soul." I'm glad these verses are in the Bible; it indicates that at times our souls need restoring and rest.

2. RECOVERY REQUIRES STAYING CLOSE TO GOD.

With all the chaos my life had become, God began to restore my soul in the stillness–the times I spent in His Word and in prayer. There was something very healing that came out of the stillness, particularly in being still and knowing that He is God (Ps. 46:10).

3. RECOVERY IS HARD WORK.

You look at the painstaking work of disaster recoveries and you can see that the work will take months or even years. I am two years out of my personal storm and I can honestly say I'm only now feeling like I'm back to my old self. Mending doesn't happen overnight. Counseling may also be necessary along the way to help work through our fragile emotions.

4. RECOVERY INVOLVES TAKING CARE OF YOU.

When everything was finally stable, I felt God saying, "You need to focus on you now." I needed a break in a big way. So I took a "mental health" vacation and went for a long weekend to visit a friend. By changing the scenery, I felt God slowly restoring my soul and re-energizing me physically. I didn't have to think about responsibilities; I could sleep in; I could have fun. As Prov. 17:22 says, "Laughter is good medicine for the soul."

5. RECOVERY REQUIRES A FRIEND WHO WILL WALK WITH YOU.

You need friends who will validate your raw emotions without judgment and spiritual answers while giving you hope; friends who will walk beside you with encouragement, prayer, and fun.

While difficult experiences can enlarge our souls, they also cut deep into our lives. Recovery creates growth–it gives our mind, body, and soul time to rejuvenate, recharge, rebuild, and repair. Let's give ourselves and others permission to recover and mend so God can make us whole again!

7

Are You Blaming Yourself for Your Prodigal?

Spotting the lies Satan tells us, and replacing guilt and pain with love.

Name Withheld

My husband and I have experienced the reality of knowing, "I have no greater joy than to hear that my children are walking in the truth"(3 John 1:4). Our two daughters professed Christ at an early age, witnessed in their schools, traveled on mission trips, and embarked into adult life with a passion for Christ. Our family life has been built around joy and laughter; and even through the teen years, we enjoyed close family times backpacking and ministering together here and abroad. The girls have been characterized as leaders, constantly encouraging and challenging those around them to live their Christian beliefs.

It always brought us great joy knowing that our children were walking in the truth. Then one bought into a lie. Now we see the flip side to the above verse: there is no greater sorrow than seeing your children walk in a lie. Since our daughter's ungodly choices, we have grieved for the loss of our close family relationships, for our witness in our community and family, over the eventual consequences of her decisions, and even grieved that God would allow this to happen. Our joy, peace, energy, and focus have been drained and replaced with despair, anger, fatigue, and distractedness. We have been plagued by questions. How could this happen? What should we do? What would influence her? How should we respond? Our close family was thrown into crisis; joy turned to sorrow, and lies twisted truth. The parable of the prodigal son has become a real and personal journey with a precious, yet prodigal, daughter.

At one point in this heavy journey, I had a mental picture of us facing our prodigal daughter, she standing with her back to us. We were pleading and begging for her to turn around, listen to God's Word, and recognize the lies. Then the focus shifted and God was standing behind me, my back turned to Him, and He was calling me to turn around and to recognize the lies. God was trying to get my attention while I was trying to get my daughter's attention. Her lies were different from mine, but nonetheless I had also been ensnared by lies. God was pleading with me to recognize and accept His truth in my own life.

God's truth needs to be sorted from the enemy's lies. I cannot allow my daughter's actions to *define* me, but I can, through God's help, allow them to *refine* me. Through godly counsel and His Word, the truth is being sifted from the enemy's subtle and pervasive lies. The refinement process is not complete, but I have identified, examined, and discarded the following lies.

LIE #1 – WHAT IF?

The enemy loves to get us into the "what if" or blame game. What if I had been more persuasive? What if I had counseled her with more studied words? What if I had been more discerning? What if I had just been a better mom? I was consumed with analyzing every nuance over the past years, reviewing my interactions, and questioning my role as both mother and wife. My analytical thoughts became paralyzing and I spiraled downward into a pit of remorse and inadequacy. Slowly through the slime, I began to see that it is not all about me. My eloquence or lack of it, my parenting skills or lack of them, will not ultimately change a heart. That is the Holy Spirit's job. I can be obedient to God's direction. I can do the best I can in parenting and counseling. But the ultimate work is God's. My pleas will not bring a prodigal into right thinking, right living, or right decisions. Our daughter made this choice in spite of Scripture, godly models, and counsel, and she will also reap the consequences of her choice. Ezekiel 18:20 reminds us that "…the son will not share the guilt of the father, nor will the father share the guilt of the son. The righteousness of the righteous man will be credited to him, and the wickedness of the wicked will be charged against him." I can neither accept the blame nor take the credit. The "what ifs" must cease because they are not from God.

LIE #2 – IF YOU PARENT WELL ENOUGH, YOUR CHILD WILL NOT MAKE UNGODLY CHOICES.

When my daughter turned away from her firm foundation, I questioned how this could happen to *my* family. Subconsciously and incorrectly, I presumed that Proverbs 22:6, "Train a child in the way he should go, and when he is old he will not turn from it" guaranteed a child's godly choices. The Lord showed me, through my own heartache, that I have wrongly judged others and their parenting ability. I thought if someone had a child not walking with the Lord, it was always a direct reflection on their parenting skills. Now on the other side with a wayward daughter, I realize the lie and repent of my judgment of others. Godly parenting does not guarantee a godly child.

LIE #3 – MY PRODIGAL ADULT CHILD DISQUALIFIES ME FOR MINISTRY.

One of the qualifications listed in 1 Timothy 3:4 for an overseer is to "manage his own family well and see that his children obey him with proper respect." This does not refer to adult children. But Satan wants to fuel our insecurities, have us focus on our inadequacies, and cripple our ministries. Instead of stepping out of ministry, we should step up to be used by God. The more open and transparent we are in our parenting journey, the more dependent we are on Him for strength, and the more opportunities there will be for us to minister. During the painful times of answering concerned inquires about our daughter, a new openness has emerged for those sharing similar burdens. One embarrassing instance of addressing pointed questions at a neighborhood party resulted in a phenomenal opportunity to share God's truth. Leadership is not about being perfect individuals. It is about being humbly obedient and available. Transparency and vulnerability can make us better servant ministers.

LIE #4 – GOD IS POWERLESS TO INTERVENE.

Somewhere in this extended battle, I crossed the line from believing God *would not* act to believing God could not act. I fell prey to the lie that God *could not* change our daughter's mind or ways. My personal systematic theology had me spinning in circles around God's sovereignty and the free will of man. The Lord had chosen to not answer my fervent prayers to radically intervene in our daughter's life. Since faith and hope are intricately entwined, I was hopeless. My view of God was too small. I do not understand how God's sovereignty and free will work, but I have become convinced that God is so much bigger than we can ever imagine. He can and will intervene if He so chooses. This mom needs to trust more, worry less, and stop trying to figure everything out. He is God and I am not! My God, our God, is a God of hope that fills us with all joy and peace as we trust in Him (Rom. 15:13), and He is more than able to do great things.

This mother's journey in parenting a prodigal is far from over. The hurt and sadness are still very real and close. But as the Lord has revealed the insidiousness of the enemy's lies, the burden has become more manageable. Now I can focus on what I am learning and not on what my daughter should be learning. This was reiterated during a recent visit. We were scheduled to rendezvous with our precious prodigal after church. The sermon was unexpectedly all too relevant: "Grace Demands a Death." The pastor pointed out that if we are to extend grace, as Christ did, we must also experience death. As parents, we need to die to our dreams, our desires, and our expectations for our children. We need to love them unconditionally, expecting nothing in return. Still stirred from this poignant message, we exited the church building and saw our daughter standing on the far side of the parking lot. My husband ran to our cold, stiff daughter, standing sullenly by the car, and wrapped her in a warm, loving hug. That was our best visit to date! My hope has been renewed; He is restoring my soul. Like Habakkuk, I will wait and keep watch from the ramparts to see what the Lord will do. God is in control and He loves us and our prodigals dearly.

8

Under His Wings

**A wife's journey of allowing God to heal heartbreak
within a broken marriage.**

by Brenda Ransom

It was date night. My husband and I were enjoying Chinese food and talking about our youngest just leaving for his freshman year of college. We had been married 26 years and I was looking forward to it being just Phil and me again. Our meal was interrupted by a call from our daughter who was temporarily living at home. She said she needed to speak to her father right away.

When we arrived home, Bethany confronted Phil with a romantic email she had found from another woman. And so began the revelation that my husband was in love with another woman and having an affair. She was from another state, so much of their romancing had been done over the computer, but they had shared a hotel room for a weekend during one of his business trips.

Surprisingly calm, I called our pastor and asked him to come right over. Our pastor was not only our friend, but my husband's boss, as he was on staff at the church as the pastor of worship. As we waited, I asked my husband the many questions flooding my mind. The immense hurt and betrayal began to set in. I was stunned that he would do this to me.

Phil moved out that night to stay with friends and had to immediately resign from his position at church and turn over his ordination certificate. I thought of having to tell our son and families. It seemed my only prayer at first was, "God, please help me get through this." A meeting with the church board and a congregational meeting where Phil would go before the church and confess his sin soon followed. A letter was sent to the entire church membership. Such a private and devastating matter now became known to hundreds of people. I no longer was a ministry wife; part of me had been taken away!

On that first Sunday, pretending I was okay, but actually dying inside, my soul ached because I knew all of these people would be hurt by this too. Yet deep in my heart, I felt the God I love begin to comfort me. When I cried at night and could not sleep, when I closed my eyes and all I could see was my husband with this other woman, I asked God to reassure me from His Word and He led me to Psalm 57:1, "Have mercy on me, O God, have mercy on me, for in you my soul takes refuge. I will take refuge in the shadow of your wings until the disaster has passed." I needed the 'shadow of His wings' for my strength and security. I asked God to help me learn from this hurt so I could use it for His glory.

Once our church knew, many of them sent cards and made loving phone calls asking, "What can we do?" They supported us through this entire trauma. God was using them to hold me up with their help and prayers because I could not stand on my own.

It was difficult to go to work each day as a teacher in a Christian school, but the staff prayed me through many difficult days. The hurt seemed unbearable, the loss overwhelming, I had no self-esteem; I felt so alone! Even so, I sensed the peace that God was giving me in all of this pain.

And so began the restoration of a marriage that needed much repair. I knew God was impressing on me to stay in the marriage. Phil wanted to stay and work on it as well.

The church set up a restoration team of men to hold my husband accountable. They were in contact with him daily. These godly men diligently prayed for and walked alongside my husband as he looked for and found a job. Several women that I chose were there for me during the restoration process as well. We met and talked often and to this day they are two of my dearest friends.

Since we hadn't been open and honest with each other for years, we had to begin. We started seeing a Christian counselor, first separately and eventually together. Phil had to face his sin head-on. Once he owned it, our counselor helped him understand how he had let our marriage unravel. I was able to share ALL of my anger, hurt, disappointment, and acknowledge my responsibility for our decline. Phil shared his feelings too and told me there were places in his life where he simply didn't trust God, even in his relationship with me. But he began to work hard to show me he wanted this to work. Phil began to leave notes in my car, text messages on my cell phone, and told me what I meant to him. He showed me he didn't want to go back to her; he wanted to stay with me. The men on the restoration team held him accountable on a day-to-day basis. As he demonstrated his renewed trustworthiness, Phil came to trust God again (that was big for me) and my trust in him slowly returned.

At times it was very sad to look back and discuss the deterioration in our marriage, but we were finally learning things and sharing inner thoughts we had kept hidden for years. We began 'dating' but I was still so hurt, many times I couldn't stay out for an entire evening with him. But we pressed on and in time we discovered:

- There was so little communication that went deep.
- There was a loss of affection physically and emotionally, and we had become very selfish.
- We did very little together; we were wrapped up in our own jobs, hobbies, and friends.
- We had become comfortable with this arrangement over time.

Could I ever forgive him? That challenge came up in counseling. After months of counseling, I began to sense the Holy Spirit nudging me to do so. Not all at once, but situation by situation. As God brought each one to me, I began to forgive and my love and respect for Phil began to grow piece by piece. Healing was taking place; I was learning things God wanted to teach me. But what haunted me the most were the pictures in my head of my husband with this woman. Finally, I began to take those thoughts captive and give them to the Lord, asking Him to replace them with a song, a Scripture verse, or a positive thought about my husband's love for me. It took so much effort and at first was so exhausting, but it worked! Even after two years, I still have to do this at times, but God has been so faithful; I will continue to trust Him with this.

After six months of separation, my husband moved back home. The dating was over, and reality had begun. Phil had a new and intentional focus that did not allow him to be passive at home anymore. I had to gradually allow him to be the head of our home. It felt new and there were times neither of us liked it much, but we were determined to live in God's strength now.

As we continue in this process, we have set up safeguards to protect what we are rebuilding:

- Our cell phones are available to each other.
- We can open the other's mail–regular or email.
- He doesn't visit computer chat rooms anymore–ever.
- We share an instant messaging ID.
- We can access each other's computer information by sharing required passwords.
- We do not use credit cards without each other's consent.
- We have joint checking and savings accounts.
- We see our counselor several times a year (proactively now) and stay in close contact with our restoration friends.
- Most importantly, we pray together every day.

It's been a process, but God has restored our marriage and family. We are resolved to not let that gradual deterioration return! My children have forgiven their father and it is so great to be together and enjoy one another again. God has renewed my husband's desire for ministry and so we wait on

Him for those opportunities.

Last September, my husband's ordination credentials were returned before the congregation that prayed for, loved, and supported us through this difficult journey these last two years. Are there still difficult days? Yes. But I know where to turn and I have found that He truly does provide that refuge in the shadow of His wings until the disaster has passed.

9

Drowning in Despair

**One woman's struggle with cancer, and how God met her
at her lowest.**

by Sarah Thebarge

On Christmas Eve of 2006, I boarded a plane in Connecticut and flew home to Chicago. My family picked me up and we drove to church for the Christmas Eve service.

I had always hoped I'd be like Mary–a young woman who loved God, whose life took an extraordinary turn. My life *had* taken an extraordinary turn, but in the wrong direction. Instead of beating the odds to become pregnant with the Messiah, I'd beaten million-to-one odds and gotten breast cancer in my 20s. And it felt like God was nowhere to be found. We began to sing Christmas carols a cappella.

Angels we have heard on high

Sweetly singing o'er the plains

And the mountains in reply

Echoing their joyous strain

Gloria, in excelsis Deo!

In excelsis Deo. I knew from my Sunday school days that the phrase was Latin for "God in the Highest." It reminded me of another Latin phrase, *in extremis.* This was a phrase I had learned in my medical training that described a patient who was struggling to breathe as they died.

As I listened to people around me singing carols, I thought, "God, I don't want you to be in the highest; I need you to be with me now in the lowest."

That's where I felt I was that Christmas: in the lowest depths. In the farthest reaches. At the point of death.

HIT WITH DEPRESSION

My mastectomy was in May, and since then I'd been in a deep depression–and December was the worst month yet.

My birthday was the second week of December and my friends threw me a dinner party to celebrate. When they brought out the cake, I closed my eyes, leaned over the candles and made a wish. Actually, it was more like a prayer. "Please, God, please don't let this year be any worse than last year was. I can't take anymore."

For months now I had felt like someone very close to me had died, and no matter how honestly and deeply I grieved, the sadness wouldn't lift. No matter how hard I tried, I couldn't shake the darkness.

And so as I thought about my birthday wish, I told God He didn't have to make my life better right away; I could probably survive as long as it didn't get any worse.

SOMEONE WHO UNDERSTANDS

The only person I could talk to about the depression was my friend Lauren, who was the adjunct professor of the first writing class I took in journalism school. She was a lifelong New Yorker who worked as an investigative reporter for a Long Island newspaper.

When I called my journalism professor to tell him I'd been diagnosed with cancer, he told me, "You should talk to Lauren." I had never talked to Lauren about anything except writing assignments.

"Why Lauren?" I asked.

"Lauren has cancer," my professor said.

A few days later, Lauren called me and asked me to meet her before class. She told me the year before she'd been diagnosed with lung cancer at the age of 37. "When I got my diagnosis, all I wanted to know was, who did I tick off in heaven?" She told me she'd been in remission for the past few months, and she was getting married the following spring, glad to be done with treatments so she could focus on reporting and the wedding.

"You'll be fine," she assured me. "I know a few women our age who kicked breast cancer's butt." The only emotion I could detect in her was anger–she was as angry at God as she imagined He was at her. I spent the first week after my diagnosis trying to explain to everyone how I felt and what I needed them to do and what I needed them not to say. I got tired of explaining, and soon I was talking to Lauren instead. She understood like no one else what it was like to have cancer and stare down the barrel of treatment and wonder if you had what it took to get through it.

Every week I took the train into New York City for classes and then the subway to Lauren's house, bringing two slices of vegetarian pizza and Cokes for dinner. She and her little terrier Bart were always waiting for me.

Then, three months before Christmas, her cancer came back. It had metastasized to her ribs and her liver and her brain. She had surgery, and then endless rounds of chemo and radiation.

NOT LOOKING FORWARD TO CHRISTMAS

As Christmas grew closer that year, Lauren and I started talking even more. Her cancer wasn't responding to treatments this time, and she was terrified of dying. My cancer was gone, but the scars on my chest ached continually. I was sleep deprived and depressed, and I spent most nights staring at the ceiling, trying to figure out what had happened to my love of Christmas.

I used to be the holiday's biggest fan. When I was in grad school, I got the Christmas tree, tied it to the top of my car, dragged it through the front door, and made my roommates help me decorate it. I made everyone get into the holiday spirit, whether they wanted to or not.

This was the first year in my life I didn't want Christmas to come. The joy that the Nativity was supposed to bring was in stark contrast to the despair I was feeling now. I thought that if the message of Christmas was true–if Jesus really had come to earth to give us joy and peace–then I wouldn't feel this low right now.

And I was feeling desperately low.

MORE BAD NEWS

Then Lauren called with more bad news. Her cancer had progressed, and her doctors told her she'd exhausted all of her treatment options.

"You're the pastor's kid; you tell me why this is happening. Isn't God supposed to show us love and compassion?"

"Well, I used to think so, but now I don't know," I answered honestly. "I mean, I wouldn't wish cancer on someone I hated, let alone someone I loved."

She told me she was going to pull the covers over her head and binge on Cheetos. "Merry f&*#ing Christmas," she said as she hung up.

The next night, I went to a holiday party where two of my friends announced they were moving out of state and another friend announced she was pregnant.

I tried to be sociable and engaging and fun, but I couldn't do it. "We have to go," I told my boyfriend.

Back at his apartment he asked, "What's the matter?"

"My friends are leaving me," I sobbed.

He pulled me close to him and rested his chin on the top of my head. "It's okay," he said. "I'll be here."

I kept crying. Finally I was able to get the words out, "And Lauren's dying," I wailed.

FIGURING OUT CHRISTMAS

My birthday wish did not come true. Instead of my 28th year being easier, it was much, much harder.

My cancer returned, and Lauren died the night before I started chemo. I missed her funeral because I was vomiting on the bathroom floor and my hair was falling out in clumps.

During my chemo sessions, I listened to carols on my iPod and tried to figure out the mystery of Christmas. I thought about how the bright lights and happy music mocked my depression and Lauren's death. How could Christmas and our pain coexist? Didn't one negate the other?

Finally, it occurred to me that maybe our pain didn't disprove the message of Christmas; maybe it validated the need for it. If the world wasn't so dark, if we weren't given to despair, if we weren't terrified of death, why would we need a Savior?

And somehow, in the midst of all the loss, I was found. God did not lift me up to the highest; He descended to me in the lowest.

As Advent approaches this year, I've been thinking that maybe the real meaning of Christmas is not *in excelsis Deo*. Our hope is not that we find God in our joy, but that He finds us in our pain.

Gloria, in extremis, Deo.

10

Grief in the Raw

Help for grieving parents and those who come alongside them.

by Lisa Elliott

We're all only one phone call away from an experience that could change our lives forever. I was at work when I received mine on August 12, 2008 at 12:40 p.m. My husband was on his way to the emergency room with our 18-year-old son Ben, who had collapsed at work.

Aside from a few minor symptoms in the previous weeks, Ben was otherwise a healthy, strong, athletic young man, the captain of the senior boys' volleyball team. He had played eighteen holes of golf with his dad three days earlier. And hadn't he just ridden his bike to work that morning? Now standing in the chemotherapy wing, my husband and I were told that there was some erratic cell behavior with the prospect of leukemia.

While my world came to a crashing halt, the world around me accelerated as blood transfusions were initiated, medication was administered, and plans were made to get Ben to the nearest cancer care treatment facility ASAP. The next day began a month's worth of in-hospital procedures to begin what was to be a two-and-a-half year treatment plan for ALL (Acute Lymphoblastic Leukemia).

Ben was put into a category all his own also having rare translocation of cells, putting him into a high risk category. This meant it was highly unlikely Ben would go into remission, and if he did he would very likely have a relapse.

We thanked God Ben went into remission one week shy of the completion of the induction phase of treatment. But by the six month marker, Ben had spent half his days in the hospital dealing with one complication after another, including three weeks over Christmas and New Year's that he didn't even remember.

On March 27, 2009, Ben underwent a bone marrow transplant. Then the unthinkable happened. Just two weeks before the transplant was scheduled, he relapsed, lessening his chances of survival. For the second time on our journey the world stood still.

Soon after, Ben had yet another relapse that led to one more month of in-hospital treatment. Unfortunately, this round of chemo was unsuccessful in achieving remission, but with this news came our biggest reality check yet—Ben had days, maybe weeks, to live. He was given a night to go home and decide between one of two options: 1) forget about any more treatment and spend the rest of his days in the hospital palliative care to keep him comfortable, or 2) go through with one final round of chemotherapy. This was an experimental chemo, unfamiliar even to our medical team, giving him a very small chance of achieving remission.

It was a decision that wasn't easy to make, but concluding a small percentage was still better than none, Ben, in typical Ben-like fashion, opted to take the chemo route. It was a valiant attempt, but was unsuccessful. After having spent two more months in the hospital, Ben decided he wanted to spend his last days in the comfort of his own bed, surrounded by the sights and sounds of home. Our last days with Ben allowed him to finish well the fight he had so bravely fought. Benjamin David Elliott was promoted to his heavenly home on August 19, 2009 at 12:35 a.m., one year and a week after his diagnosis.

We are sad beyond words with the loss of our son and feel his life with us was far too short. But the impact of his life and the Christ-like attitude he carried to his death have been far-reaching. A message he shared with our church family only ten days before he died has been said to be "the best sermon ever heard." It can be viewed on YouTube (enter Ben Elliott, Stratford).

Many, including complete strangers, joined our journey of faith through a Facebook page, "The Ben Ripple." It soon became a venue for people to not only enter into the life of our family but also reap some "BENefits" of their own as they related it to their own lives.

One thing that came out of our journey is a GriefShare group. One of the exercises encouraged us to write a letter to family and friends to express what our current state of grief is like and to inform them of what they can expect of us through this time. I shared mine, and afterward the consensus was that I should share my letter beyond the class in case someone out there might be struggling to understand the effects of grief. The letter is entitled "My Grief in the Raw."

Dear Family and Friends,

I thank you for your love and support throughout Ben's illness and subsequent death. It means so much to me knowing you've carried me and my family to Jesus over and over again on your knees in prayer.

It's hard to imagine that it's been seven months since Ben changed addresses from his temporal home to his eternal home. It seems at times that it was just yesterday that he was running through the door on his way out again. And hence, it's still hard to believe that he is now gone and that there will no longer be memories that include him.

I know that it must be so painful for you to watch me in pain. I realize you may be at a loss for words or feel inadequate to reach into my pain. No doubt there are times when you feel awkward around me as I shed tears or at other times when I seem unresponsive to your attempts to somehow make me feel better. I thank you for your patience when in my raw state of grief I may respond harshly to you. I apologize if I in any way have hurt you as I've worked through my grief.

I'm tired and easily distracted. I don't have a lot of social energy right now. In fact, I often feel like a caged animal looking for a quick escape route in social settings. I am sad, but I'm not looking for anyone to make me happy. I am broken, but I'm not looking for anyone to fix me. I am not looking for answers. I am not looking for sympathy. I need people to be okay with my sadness, realizing that my tears are bringing healing. I need people to be more interested in entering into my pain than trying to get me to the other side of it.

As much as I appreciate the loving motive behind them, assurances that "One day it'll all make sense" or "One day you'll feel better" only serve to project a future I can't make sense of yet. Words such as "Ben's in a better place" or "Ben isn't suffering any longer" don't bring the comfort that I'm seeking, but rather simply remind me of what I already know. Although they hold elements of truth, words intended to help me "Look at the bright side" make me feel that somehow I'm living "on the dark side." Words that encourage me to "Think of all I have to be thankful for," usually beginning with "Well, at least..." only suit to minimize my pain and imply that I'm not thankful for what I do have. Words cheapen my pain. Answers to questions I'm not asking frustrate me.

Be assured that there have been moments where there is a vaguely recognizable sense of relief. I like how Ben's girlfriend described it. She said, "It's like coming up for air. It's like most of the time we're in the ocean and every once in a while we come up and take a quick breath of air before being submerged again." That revelation in and of itself was refreshing! Because, yes, grief can sometimes swallow you whole and suck the breath out of you!

I think all of us concerned have done well to "go on living life" even when it hurts. Just as God's grace sustained me and my family throughout Ben's illness, I know He will continue to do so now in our grief. God has strengthened us all to "do the next thing," whatever that has been along the way. It might amount to something as simple as taking a walk or having an extra cup of tea or just hanging out together as a family. God is comforting me with His quiet presence. He is holding my hand as He's guiding my steps. He is entering into my pain rather than seeking to get me over it. My pain is what God is using to reach deep into the recesses of my heart where He alone can speak powerful words of truth and comfort. I believe He is using my pain for His glory as I share my journey with others.

I don't know what "being okay" will look like for me personally. But I do know that I will not always feel as I do now. I know that laughter and joy will emerge again someday. And I do know that I will survive and eventually recover. I cling to that knowledge, even though there are times when I don't feel it. And I trust that I will be a better person, becoming more like Jesus as a result.

Please pray that I would come to see meaning in my loss and that God would continue to teach me valuable lessons in my pain. Please feel free to talk about Ben and don't be afraid of our tears when you do. We long to hear mention of his name. We want to know that his life and his death are still making an impact for the Kingdom of God. We want to know that he's not forgotten. Most of the time, given the right time and place, we are bursting to share our all-consuming thoughts with anyone who will give ear.

Thank you for caring about me and my family. Thank you for listening to me with no words. Thank you for validating my pain by simply crying with me. Thank you for understanding when I've seemed distant or aloof or disengaged or uninterested in your life. Thank you for giving me the necessary time and space to work through my grief. Thank you for not giving up on me.

And finally, "Praise be to the God and Father of our Lord Jesus Christ, the Father of compassion and the God of all comfort, who comforts us in all our troubles, so that we can comfort those in any trouble with the comfort we ourselves have received from God" (2 Cor. 1:3-4).

Lisa (Mom)

~ Author Biographies ~

Tammy Kill is a hospice nurse. She is actively involved as a children's ministry leader and enjoys singing and writing. She and her husband have eight children. They live in Lima, Ohio.

Jill Briscoe is a popular writer and conference speaker who has authored over fifty books and travels all over the world. Jill is executive editor of *Just Between Us*, a magazine encouraging and equipping women for a life of faith. Jill and her husband, Stuart, have been in ministry for over 50 years and have a worldwide radio ministry, *Telling the Truth*. She and her husband live in suburban Milwaukee, Wisconsin, have three grown children, and thirteen grandchildren.

Shelly Esser has been the editor of *Just Between Us*, a magazine encouraging and equipping women for a life of faith, for the last 25 years. She is an author and has written numerous articles. She and her husband live in southeastern Wisconsin. They have four daughters and a son-in-law.

Nancy Nordenson is the author of *Just Think: Nourish Your Mind to Feed Your Soul* (Baker) and *Finding Livelihood: A Progress of Work and Leisure* (Kalos Press). Her essays have appeared in a variety of publications. She and her husband live in Minneapolis, Minnesota.

Susie O'Berski is the author of the book, *We Are the Much More*. She and her husband have five sons, three daughters-in-law, and seven grandchildren. They live in Ft. Myers, Florida.

Brenda Ransom and her husband live in the Milwaukee area in Wisconsin. They have two adult children and three grandchildren.

Sarah Thebarge is a speaker at retreats, colleges, and conferences. She is also an author. Her memoir, *The Invisible Girls*, was published by Jericho Books in 2013. Additionally, she earned a degree in medical science from Yale. She was studying Journalism at Columbia University when she was diagnosed with breast cancer at age 27. Sarah lives in Santa Barbara, California.

Lisa Elliott is a pastor's wife, mother, speaker, and award-winning author of *The Ben Ripple* and *Dancing in the Rain*. She and her husband, David, live in London, Ontario, have four children (one in heaven), and a grandson. Visit Lisa at lisaelliottstraightfromthe heart.webs.com.

"*JBU* has been my lifeline for over 25 years! It's like having coffee with a best friend who knows what it's like to live a life of faith."

- Pam Farrel
Speaker & Author

Spiritual Refreshment
You'll find that and more in the pages of *Just Between Us*.

Join other women from around the world and become part of the *Just Between Us* family like Pam Farrel. You'll love this inspiring quarterly magazine filled with biblicaly-based articles that will encourage and lift your soul.

Subscribe for the special price of $14.95!

ORDER TODAY for yourself, a friend, or a ministry partner at justbetweenus.org/ BestofJBU or call 800-260-3342. This offer applies to U.S. subscribers only.

Made in the USA
San Bernardino, CA
09 March 2016